Money System Gone Insane

How to Benefit from the Rise of Digital Currencies in The Coming Financial Crisis

Risto Pietilä, The Dragon

To accompany the book, we are releasing the keynote videos from Barcelona to the first 200 who buy the book. To see if you qualify, go to:
www.dragonspeaks.io/keynote

Contents

Introduction

An ever-increasing disgruntlement in the money system in the world spawned this book. This "System" with greed in its core is wrong on so many levels, and it is time someone tackled the issue head on.

It wasn't just that certain top elites were exploiting the poor and the middle class. It was that they rigged the game in a way that left the majority at a great loss.

For years, I've spoken on issues covered in this book, written on forums and tried to help others see what I see.

I mean, I haven't just been rallying others to complain with me; I've explained how the money system works, and how to use it for your advantage. When more and more people "get it," perhaps we can do something about it—together.

...

Throughout the history of man, those hungry for power have tried to suppress others. I'm not just talking about bullying at school or at the workplace; it goes much further.

If you look at the society now, at the beginning of the year 2020, there are many suppressing factors prevalent in it.

We call this arrangement the "System." Some main aspects of the System are:

- The debt-based monetary system
- Society's many forms of inequality, poverty, need, and hunger
- The systemic threat of actual violence and terror, war

But that is not all. When you dig deeper, you will come across the System's way of

- Indoctrination and propaganda, perversion of truth and wisdom
- Suppression of advanced technologies
- Suppression of human development, especially regarding mental and spiritual understanding

For most people, living in the System creates a stranglehold over their life. As a result, they view themselves paralyzed and trapped.

Even though western societies (or any other ones) can celebrate historically high quality of life, most people are worried, stressed, and frustrated.

Many people cannot easily dream of a life that makes sense. Yet this life is found in books and tales, and many prophecies in various religions and traditions.

Some can and want to dream of such a way of life becoming a reality again. They are, however, marginalized in the society that is strongly under the suffocating control of the System.

Lately, starting after the second world war and constantly speeding up in pace, people have grown in their awareness and understanding of world events. There is real-time access to more news reports than one can ever consume.

One could even speak of a developmental change in human consciousness, regarding having access and being aware of great volumes of information.

At the same time, the global population has increased. This has created a situation where thousands of people have a deep understanding about various aspects of how the world works, and millions have woken up to a significant degree.

The advances of information and communications technology (ICT), namely the Internet, mobile phone, and later, smartphone, have brought all the people and all the knowledge of the world to be instantly accessible to billions.

Startups and cryptocurrencies have given more financial resources to the hands of those wanting global change to happen. Also, in other sectors of life we've seen lots of improvement.

I believe we are at the brink of the System's collapse. It is about to fall.

With that shift, only the aspects of society that no longer serve best interest of the collective will fall away. The markets and industries which make the modern world a marvel will continue to develop as long as humans have free will.

...

In this book, I endeavor to shed some light on the economic and monetary aspects of the shift we have at hand.

The main contents stem from my keynote talk held in Barcelona, Spain in August 2019. This was an invitation-only seminar I held for a close mastermind group.

The participants comprised an international group composed of both bright economic thinkers, key players in the Bitcoin ecosystem, and other chosen participants representing fields such as gamification, tech, and viral marketing and media.

...

What I want you to get from this book is how money works. I will touch upon the problems of the current banking system and the cartelized strangle-hold inherent to the most popular currencies, such as US Dollar and Euro.

This book is philosophical at its core. It explains the underlying structure and principles that govern money creation, the rapid expansion of cryptocurrencies, and the premises of programming global solutions.

I intend this book for people who seek more information on questions such as

- What is the world's current monetary system's foundation?
- Where does money come from and how is it created?
- What made Bitcoin such an innovation among currencies and different assets?
- What are the limitations of Bitcoin and other currently available crypto coins (or "altcoins" as in "alternative crypto currencies other than Bitcoin")?
- How is the "efficiency of code" a key factor in changing our currency?
- How can we introduce a world-wide currency that "really works"?

When you understand the money system, you will be an early adopter when the platform changes. And to understand this system, you need to know how money is created and what we would need to have a better platform or regime in the current one's place. Then, when you understand the different ways how to change the platform, you can be one of the change makers.

For those who are not familiar with me, it may suffice to say here that I was a serial entrepreneur and self-made millionaire before I ever invested in Bitcoin. But with Bitcoin and later with Monero, I attained total financial freedom and became what some might call an "Angel investor," or a "Bitcoin whale."

I dislike both labels. If you must call me something, call me the "Dragon." (I'll be very pleased if you do.)

God has gifted me with a brain that is well suited for economic thinking. I enjoy the modelling, the concepts and the far-reaching impact of economic thoughts. (My other professor chair is in Theology. I am also a decent singer.)

I started stock investing in my teen-age years, founded and co-founded several companies in my twenties, and became a millionaire before I was thirty. Perhaps having an economist's brain helped me to predict how the prices of certain stocks, precious metals and crypto currencies developed—and to profit from this understanding.

But no individual can experience deep fulfillment from how much money they have. Yes, becoming financially free is great; it means I'm not bound by "work" and its obligations that would enslave me all day.

The fulfillment one gets from personal wealth is only minor. True wealth is when you set other people free. I felt the burden of seeing others enslaved by money—and the underlying financial structures.

Some may call me eccentric. Others would label me plain crazy. Well, anyone passionate about economics and cryptocurrencies has to be a bit crazy. That is a given!

But, as you'll find out as you read the book, I have a unique take on the economic situation in the world. I've been correct numerous times with my economic predictions, that different notable publications have quoted.

...

For someone who is new to cryptocurrencies, this will be an easy-to-read introduction to the underlying factors that contribute to the inevitable demise of fiat currencies.

Even if you are well-versed in Bitcoin, Blockchain, and all the rest, I can promise you several new realizations just by reading this book.

In fact, if you read this book and can honestly say there was nothing new to you, I'll be happy to refund your purchase—or buy you any economic book of your choosing!

Block out all interruptions for the next hour or so. Take this time to let my words sink in. I promise you; I'll be respectful of your time and be concise.

I love to hear from my readers. To get in touch with me and to connect with the people who are making the principles laid out in this book a reality, please go to my personal website www.dragonspeaks.io.

At the end of this book, I have a special gift for those who've read it. But now, please turn off your cellphone and take the next hour as I lead you through the rabbit hole...

Part 1 – A New Money System of the 2020s

The problem of debt

The question is: How to overthrow this dominant system, where the currency is created out of debt?

The world as we know it is run by a "fiat money system." If the term is new to you, let me briefly quote one definition:

"Fiat money is a currency without intrinsic value that has been established as money, often by government regulation. Fiat money does not have use value and has value only because a government maintains its value, or because parties engaging in exchange agree on its value."[1]

Ever since Richard Nixon, the 37th President of the United States, decoupled the US dollar from the gold standard in 1971, we've seen a rise of national fiat money systems around the world. Today it is the dominant paradigm.

The problem is that the fiat money system creates new money through debt. This "fiat money system" is at the same time an ingenious as well a very evil way of organizing the platform we base our money on.

I saw this problem early on around 2005. Even before I understood exactly how the System

---

[1] For a layman's explanation, see:
https://en.wikipedia.org/wiki/Fiat_money

functions, I knew that it was hindering the progress of mankind. In the back of my mind, I knew that this system should be dissolved and overthrown.

This is no easy feat. Everybody who has tried to meddle with the money system, let alone purposefully seek to dissolve and overthrow it, has been murdered.

The prime example of this is president John F. Kennedy, "JFK," who challenged and looked to demolish the privately controlled central banking system in the US.

In 2005, my vision was still very limited. It was clear to me, however, that the money system had started to go in the wrong direction with the absolution of the gold standard. To remedy the situation, I was also looking to find an answer from the physical realm.

Therefore, I tried to find a physical way, some kind of natural law that, when applied would, dethrone the system and allow us to build a new one.

At that point in time, I found silver to be the way to achieve this goal. I spoke at length of this revelation in my earlier book, a treatise written in Finnish of silver as an investment and an economic instrument.[2]

---

[2] Risto Pietilä: Sijoitushopea Suomessa (in Finnish, translates to "Investment Silver in Finland"). Originally

In essence, there were several deep monetary and economic revelations I had at the time. I saw the benefits of the gold standard or silver standard.

As profound as those realizations were at the time, there is no need to expound on them here, because they have since become obsolete. But I will revisit some of them briefly here, for the sake of the story.

If there were no cryptocurrencies, then silver would have been "the way." I believed it was the best physical way to get the power back to the people.

At the time, my goal was twofold. First, I aimed to show and verify the shortage of silver. Second, I sought to monetize the silver that was already in people's hands in a distributed way.

To understand the preference of silver over gold, it is good to understand that gold had huge monetary stocks that were, nominally, in the hands of several governments.

But, in actuality, the governments were not in control of the gold. The bankers were.

The situation was different with silver. The bankers had two very different strategies for how to make these precious metals not able to function as money.

---

published 2010.

With gold, they collected it from the hands of the people and concentrated it in places like Fort Knox. Then, they stole it and took the gold to the bankers' private vaults.

So, gold was dethroned through theft.

Silver, on the contrary, was dethroned by the exact opposite: by dispersing it to the people and even to industrial applications. With this, silver became commoditized as well as too volatile to be used effectively as a currency.

I could, of course, write at length here on silver and the monetary economics related to it. That, however, would be beside the point.

Yes, I had spent years in achieving this understanding. Yes, silver at the time appeared as the best remedy to the rotten situation. But then there was a disruption.

The emergence of cryptocurrencies clearly showed that the battle for monetary dominance is no longer fought in the physical domain. The battlefield is in the virtual domain.

The fiat money system has, of course, always been virtual. Sure, it may have had printed certificates that in effect say, "this represents an amount of fiat money." That physical representation, emblem or token does not, however, make it less virtual. It is just a printed token.

With the benefit of hindsight, I find it amusing that at the time I was looking back in history for a solution to the problems in the present time. I thought the problems of virtual money, and a treacherous fiat money system, in particular, could be solved by going back to physical money, such as gold or silver.

I was wrong. The solution was not to go back but to move forward, just more aggressively.

The source of the problem was virtual money created out of debt. But the solution would be virtual money without debt.

In a sense, it is not just a question of "fighting your enemy with their weapons."

If you are armed with chariots, and an opponent develops a fighter plane to attack and torment you, what do you do? Sure, you can counter your enemy by rising to their level. If they attack you with a fighter plane, you counter them with an anti-aircraft defense or a better fighter.

In other words, you can have a solution on the earth's level or the aerial level. But it is better to go higher. You counter your enemy from a level they can't function in.

With the example above, you go to the space level. This could mean having a mother ship in space. It is an unseen threat to the enemy fighter. It spots the attacking fighter plane and can demolish it unexpectedly.

This, in effect, is what happened with the advent of cryptocurrencies.

An asset class of its own

Concerning economic and monetary theory, the striking fact with cryptocurrencies is that they are something new.

I saw early on, that cryptocurrencies presented a new asset class for the first time since the common stock 500 years ago. In such a long time, no one had managed to create a new one... Not until Bitcoin.

Theoretically, we don't have that many asset classes. These, of course, depend on what kind of classification we make.

The easiest way to classify between physical asset classes is between movable and immovable things. Of course, we have the traditional "monies," gold and silver.

Of course, in some cultures and certain periods, something else may have functioned as money such as grain, salt, copper, animal skins or whatever.

But, to make this as simple as possible, we can say that the basic asset classes are:

1. Physical money
2. Things
3. Land and the immovable things built on it, such as buildings and structures of different kinds

These were the origins of asset classes. Then, when we think about virtual assets, there were the debt instruments and shares of companies or shares of common stock or something similar.

These shares, of course, differ from physical objects because they represent an entitlement to something. Debt, in a sense, is an entitlement to a future flow of liquid money.

But these asset classes have existed for a long time.

With cryptocurrencies, for the first time in centuries or millennia, someone created a new asset class.

What, then, makes cryptocurrency a "new asset class?"

This is a fact that most people failed to recognize (and that still is not commonly known). The uniqueness of cryptocurrencies lies in that they created something that is virtual but does not have a counterparty.

In a sense, both debt and equity have a counterparty. In both, someone has to deliver to you, or they will be liable for it. Strictly speaking, however, equity does not have "a" counterparty (because nobody is liable to pay) but it requires a societal arrangement where claims can be enforced.

Even more so, with cryptocurrencies there is no counterparty. They have nothing that someone else would need to deliver. Yet they are not physical but virtual.

This is something that did not exist before and, to my knowledge at least, it hasn't ever existed anywhere.

So, from our perspective, such an asset class didn't exist until Satoshi showed it in 2008 and until the Bitcoin network was started in 2009.

This was a monumental thing. And in the beginning, it was missed by almost everybody.

What followed, with time, was the first "Bitcoin maximalist craze," then the "altcoin craze," and, after a while, "blockchain" became the buzzword on everybody's lips.

The pattern behind all these innovations is very similar. First, people approach this phenomenon from different angles, which spawn their different buzzwords, even with elements of mania. As a result, we see people organizing "blockchain events," or creating multiple altcoins with no real purpose whatsoever. Others then will venture to put out "app coins," or whatnot.

Yet, from the perspective of monetary theory, nothing novel has come after Bitcoin. It's the same old rehashed in a different package.

The relevant novelty factors, from the viewpoint of monetary theory, is having something virtual without a liable counterparty.

So, Bitcoin is still the biggest cryptocoin by market capitalization. And the reason is that its creation was the most fundamental event, and it hasn't been surpassed by anything.

Why is this? The basic reason is that all those other coins that have been created after Bitcoin, don't solve a problem that would be more valuable or more fundamental than the one Bitcoin is solving.

Money – where do you come from?

Let's consider for a moment how money is created. For every currency one needs to specify, how new money is introduced to the system. In other words, what structure or construct determines, on an annual basis, how new money comes into something like a society, and how it is distributed.

To answer such a question, we can think of all the possible answers. But, for the sake of brevity, let's start with the one that is currently at use.

In the fiat money system, new money is created by commercial banks. They, however, can't just print money at will. There has to be someone who wants to borrow money from the banks. This is a feature of the current system that money can't just be printed at will when the bank should feel so.

Some may say that the current monetary system is based on "printing money out of thin air." In a way, this is not true because even "printing the money out of thin air" would be much preferable to the current system.

The current system is far worse. In it, money is created against a promise to pay back with interest. This may sound innocuous, but it is far from it.

The money taken as debt is created into the system, but the interest needed for the payback is not. That interest is never created but has to come from within the economy.

Let that one sink in for a moment. Where does that money come from?

To shed some light over the situation, let's look at an example. When you enter into a debt contract with a commercial bank, you promise to pay the money back with interest.

Perhaps you take a mortgage or something similar. You need €100,000 to buy a house.

With the mortgage, you take on yourself an obligation to pay back €200,000 back to the bank over 30 years.

The funny thing is–and when you think of it, it is not funny at all–that the €100,000 was created at the moment when you took on this contract, but the other €100,000 is not created and never will be created.

Yet you are liable to pay the bank that money. You have to pay the bank something that does not exist, that you don't have and that will never be created into the economy.

This is a very well-designed structure. It is a means of enslavement that keeps everybody in the current monetary system in a stranglehold. Through this mechanism, the banker-controlled system strangles the economy, the people, and the planet itself.

Why? Because this debt structure makes it impossible to fulfill what it forces people to do to live. So, it forces everybody to enter into impossible contracts. It tricks them into obligations that cannot be fulfilled, and it doesn't provide any means of fulfilling them.

By this, the money system holds people responsible in an impossible contract. When people fail, the money system, through banks, collects the people's assets, such as these houses, that then become the property of those banks.

So, of course, the houses don't disappear. When this system has been enforced, a lot of physical assets–even wealth–have been constructed. But at the same time, the system is incredibly coercive because participation is forced. If you would wish not to participate in it, you are not given that option.

It may be new to you, but it is close to impossible not to engage the fiat money system. Especially in any western society, it's difficult to even live your life without taking on debt. Very few people manage to do so.

In Finland, you have a clean credit record if you have always paid back according to the schedule, if ever you have taken debt in the first place. In the U.S. it is worse: people that are seeking to be debt-free actually suffer from a lousy credit record for not willing to participate in the system. This has implications beyond just borrowing.

It is just a mathematical fact that you are forced into debt. For you to have any money whatsoever in your account, it means that somebody else has to be in debt.

The amount of debt in the world exceeds the amount of money in circulation. Furthermore, it is not just that "there is a bit more debt than actual money." We're talking of multiples.

This debt-system has been in operation for over a hundred years. The consequences are drastic.

In my opinion, it is the greatest crime perpetrated on mankind. In comparison, all wars and genocides are a lesser evil.

I will attempt to explain this through the example of a well-known board game.

Lessons from "Monopoly"

The classic board game Monopoly was a parody game from the get-go. The game starts with the bank owning all the property and most of the money. The players then seek to purchase those properties and accumulate their wealth.

Why do I call it a "parody game?" In the real world, the system is rigged so that in the end, the banks will own everything.

Monopoly first came out in the 1930s in the US, at a time when the debt-money system had already been operating for 20 years. During that time, the debt-money system had created a huge market bubble and subsequent (and inevitable) crash, that forced multitudes to sell their properties to banks.

For this reason, I call the original Monopoly board game a parody game from the beginning on. The upside in the game, of course, is that you at least start with some money.

If, however, you want to play a *realistic* Monopoly, it would go the opposite way. The game starts with the players owning the properties instead of the bank. The properties would be fully developed, too.

But the players would have no money at all. To get any funds, the players would need to take on loans or other debt instruments from the bank – and pay back with interest.

This way, the game starts literally with the players with no money yet owning all the properties. Then, when you move in the game and hit someone's property, you pay the owner rent according to the going price.

You don't have the money just because you don't. The Central Bank, such as the Federal Reserve, which is a private bank, has a monopoly on creating money.

Then, to pay your rent, you contract a debt from the bank, pay what you owe to your neighbor, and then the turn passes on. Soon all the players will end up in a situation where none of you has any money or any properties.

The only one that can win in this setting, mathematically, is the bank.

This is not just "science fiction." It is the true "Monopoly" that has been played out on us for the last 106 years, at a minimum.

Why 106 years? Well, it is ever since the Federal Reserve Act was passed by the US Congress and signed into law by President Woodrow Wilson on December 23, 1913. This law created the central banking system of the United States, known as the Federal Reserve System.

During the 20th century, this same fiat money system spread globally.

So, let's sum up the basic definition of the fiat money system through the mechanism used to create new money. How is money created? New money comes into the economy through the people's willingness to take on debt and with a promise to pay it back to the bank with interest.

If you are heavily "in the system" yourself, it may be difficult to see the situation. But keep reading. You are a little short of an epiphany.

To help you with a different perspective, let me share my account as someone shunned by the banks with regard to getting a loan.

Why I can't get a loan?

Getting a loan is the basis of this money system. If you wish to cut someone out, you don't allow them to get a loan.

What is peculiar is that getting a loan is something that many ordinary people cannot do anymore.

I have long ago passed the point when banks would want to finance anything that I do. For example, if I were to go to the bank and ask to get a loan for any kind of purpose, I would not get it. Regardless of whatever kind of collateral I would provide, I would not get it.

At some point, I even offered, as a guarantee, to deposit double the amount in physical gold in the bank vault. Still, I would not get the loan.

So, in practical terms, this means two kilos of physical gold for every 30,000 Euros. But still, my application would not go through.

For this reason, people who would have some profitable ideas to pursue, are unable to get the loans they seek. The only ones who can get a loan are the ones who play according to the bank's rule book, don't ask it for purposes that create anything and don't provide any value.

Why governments are sure to get a loan

With normal people, getting a loan is limited to only "those who meet these criteria." With the governments, on the other, the situation is the opposite.

Governments always get a loan because this is what the international banks want anyway. When a government is going deeper into debt, it is going deeper and deeper into the stranglehold of the banks.

That's why all the governments, are not only able to get debt but they are also forced to do so, too. That is the actual goal. The reason is control.

Let's take some modern examples. Today, the government of Libya, for example, is running deeper and deeper into debt. When Gaddafi was in power, they had no debt whatsoever.

Or let's look at Finland. After World War II, Finland experienced an economic miracle against all odds.

This is something I would like to explain in more detail, as Finland is my native country.

The rise and fall of after-WW2 Finland

So, let's cover the history of Finland from the aftermath of the Second World War (WW2) to 1990s.

First, because Finland lost the war, it had to pay war reparations. In monetary terms, Finland's war reparations to the Soviet Union were originally worth US$300,000,000 at 1938 prices. Yes, you read it right – Finland owed the USSR 300 Million US dollars.

A decade later, in 1948, the sum was cut down by a quarter to "just" $226,500,000. That is a huge sum. Yet it would mean even more in today's currency. When you take inflation into account, that $300 Million adds up to over $4 Billion in the currency of 2019.

But the price Finland had to pay was not purely financial.

On top of these massive debts, Finland lost 35 000 square kilometers of land to the Soviet Union. These land areas also included one of Finland's industrial heartlands and the second-largest city, Viipuri.

To put this into perspective: Finland wasn't an industrialized country before the war, to begin with, and still, it lost a good part of the industry it had had before the war.

Of course, the lost areas affected a lot of people, too. Nearly 430,000 Karelians, approximately 12% of the population, lost their homes and needed to be relocated.

Yet, after the war, Finland experienced rapid economic growth. Besides economic development, also both social and political stability increased considerably in the next decades.

In a matter of three decades, Finland saw a turn from a war-ravaged agrarian society into a "heaven on earth," becoming one of the most technologically advanced countries in the world, with a sophisticated market economy and several strong industries, and its inhabitants enjoying a relatively high standard of living.

Politically, there was a big shift, however, when the longstanding President Kekkonen (in office from 1956 to 1982) relinquished power.

That marked a significant turn in the financial politics of the country. All of a sudden, Finland wanted to "integrate with the western financial system." This, of course, is a euphemism for giving away your sovereignty.

What this integration means, in practice, is that first you give away all your gold, and then you give away your power to create money for the benefit of your people. And you loan money from international banks.

Eventually, all the benefits go to the international banks instead of your people. And then you have to start paying your debtors interest on the debt.

For reasons that are beyond me, Finland wanted to have international banks create the money and take it as debt rather than create the money on its own. It is pure craziness.

But the propaganda for this "integration" is so powerful. The schoolbooks say that when you need to borrow all your money from somebody else, it is in fact "a proof of stability" and whatnot.

If it says so in print, even in the esteemed schoolbooks, then it must be so. Even governments have to adhere to schoolbooks. I mean, how could a schoolbook ever lie? If it is part of mandatory education, something that everybody in the country must read, how could it be even possible for it not to be true?

Please allow me my sarcasm.

Studying money creation

My original goal was to outline what are the theoretical possibilities of how the money could be created on an annual basis. Knowing these, you can create money.

It's easy to get started with gold and silver.

When physical gold was used as money, nobody had any say over it. If you go and mine some gold, then, in a sense, more gold is created. The reason for this is that when more gold is refined, then the monetary stock is augmented with the amount of a new creation.

With paper money, money is created through debt. This was already covered earlier in detail.

With cryptocurrencies, such as Bitcoin, we speak of algorithmic creation. This means, there is no individual, no human, who decides over it.

In Bitcoin, as an example, new Bitcoins are created through "Bitcoin mining." The algorithm, in essence, would say that "Okay, this many Bitcoins are up for grabs this year and if you participate in mining, you get your share."

Here we can draw an analogy between gold mining and Bitcoin mining. During gold times, in a sense, the more effort you put into mining, the more you would get.

Then, of course, money may be created out of thin air. It's not just a theoretical possibility; this has actually happened. That was the case, for example, with Finland or any other independent country that printed their own money.

That is what a sovereign nation does: It prints its own money and decides how to spend it.

In this context of nation-states, the government has an established legitimacy to the people, kind of.

Most people, especially in western countries, when you think about to what they belong to, they usually feel that they belong to themselves and often they belong to a family, but much less to a tribe. However, quite often they feel they belong to their nation.

For example, the Finnish people identify more with Finland than with their own family. And between family and the nation, there is very seldom anything to identify with.

Of course, in Europe and many other places, the "nation-state" does not always coincide with "nation," because many nations are in fact occupied by "nation-states," such as Catalonia in Spain. They refer to the Madrid administration as "Castilians," a separate nation that is unlawfully holding sway over them.

Europe is full of movements to establish wider autonomy or full independence for such peoples such as the Catalans. Similarly, you'll find other nations occupied by nation-states.

But even those nations who consider themselves occupied or oppressed, still one way or another identify with the nation-state.

So, in this context, the government has a certain natural foundation of legitimacy to run such a scheme on its people. People trust that the government issued banknotes have value based on what is printed on the papers, the same as the digits that exchange ownership digitally.

But, if you think about the global level, the goal is to go beyond nation-states. The people behind this scheme are trying to create global governments or global authorities that would be able to overstate the national authorities or people's authority and thinking.

The challenge here is that people don't feel that these self-appointed global so-called authorities are legitimate. And the problem, of course, is that they are self-appointed.

Take, for example, the governance structure of the European Union. It is a carefully crafted mess. It is a mess carefully designed to hide the fact that it is a corporation working for entirely something else than in the European People's benefits. All the elections and procedures are completely bogus. In reality, they have nothing to do with actual decision making.

People call "bullshit!" if they are being presented
with some global organizations pretending to be
legitimate and the "binding agreements."

People see through all those. They just say, "Hey, I
haven't submitted to this. Perhaps the elected
officials of my country gave their go-ahead, but even
that was illegal."

Obviously, when you have to do things illegally, it
means that there is something shady with them.
This is exactly the situation with the European
Union and the Euro system. They were all instigated
illegally. However, as this is not my main point here,
I won't write more on that here.

Let's, instead, look at other means of creating
legitimacy and trust.

There is the technical possibility that we have a
legitimate committee, not a self-appointed one, that
enjoys the trust of the people and then decides
about monetary matters. But this is of course only a
theoretical possibility because the concept of
legitimacy is, in fact, a difficult one.

Earlier in history, it was easier because the
government was an extension of God. Thus, the
monarch ruled her land, because, by the grace of
God, she was the Queen of England.

If someone were to question her authority and say,
"Hey, what makes you the Queen of England!?"

The reply would just be, "By the grace of God, I am the Queen of England. That makes me the fount of honor. All government stems from me because I have my position by the grace of God."

End of discussion. The answer was exhaustive. If you object, please continue the dialogue with the armed guards in their quarters and the bricks of the Tower prison.

Nowadays, it is more difficult. To establish legitimacy, one is forced to reach an agreement on issues such as "who counts as a human."

The Finnish constitution says, according to the official English translation, "The powers of the State in Finland are vested in the people, who are represented by the Parliament."[3]

This means, the authority and power in the State of Finland, springs up from the people. It is vested in the people.

But who are the people? How do you define them?

---

[3] In the original Finnish, it is worded: ""Valtiovalta Suomessa kuuluu kansalle, jota edustaa valtiopäiville kokoontunut eduskunta." The Constitution of Finland, available at: https://www.finlex.fi/en/laki/kaannokset/1999/en1999 0731.pdf

The definitions of "who counts as a member of the people" and "how many votes should the people have" are completely arbitrary.

Yet, both in the US and in Finland, only a person who is 18 or older by a set date can vote in an election. Another person who at the set date is 17 years, 364 days, 23 hours and 59 minutes old, can't vote.

In both the US and Finland, those people who would be eligible to vote but don't, effectively don't have a vote. Their non-participation cancels their say in that vote.

In federal elections, only citizens can vote. But there are some local elections where non-citizens such as illegal immigrants can vote.

When considering how many votes you have, your possessions are not considered. Someone, who has paid millions of Euros or Dollars in taxes to their country, will not get more votes. That person has the same one vote as a person who is receiving their whole income in state benefits.

In a sense, all such decisions and definitions are arbitrary. But let me look at this from a different point of view.

Where does legitimacy come from? In a sense, we have two sources of governmental legitimacy and power. One is from "above" or from God and the other one is from "the grassroots" or the people.

Both of these have insurmountable problems. Anyone can say they are sent by God. But if the person is not from God, then he or she is essentially using the people towards his or her own goals, because there is no agreeable basis on the legitimacy that is somehow springing from the people.

So how do we do this with money? If the money is a people's venture, it means that you just cannot find an agreement. But if the money is a godly venture, then it means that you have to either force it on people or you need to let the people choose it voluntarily.

At the moment we are very much in the situation that we have a monetary system that is forced on people. On the other hand, Bitcoin is an example of a monetary system that is not forced on anyone. People have chosen to adopt it.

Bitcoin is doing very well, especially for those people who participated in it early on. For example, back in 2010, when I was first discussing Bitcoin in my club in Helsinki, the going rate for Bitcoin was less than $1 per Bitcoin.

From an investment perspective, Bitcoin has been a spectacular investment, having gone up in its appreciation to more than 10,000 times in just a few years.

Bitcoin is, as I stated earlier, something that for the first time in history (that I know of at least) has produced such innovation in monetary theory and practice.

To, again, look at the issue from a different point of view, let's consider for a moment, what makes Bitcoin such a great innovation.

Part 2 – It is time for a revolution!

Spreading of Innovations

Let's take a simple example to study how innovations spread. First, you have an invention with great potential. Let's take "fire" as our example.

A common storyline about "how fire was developed" is that somebody found it by accident, but then learned that it was useful, and therefore continued to develop ways to produce it at will to cause it to happen consistently. After that, it just spread to all the people because it was so useful and greatly benefited those adopting it.

Fire spread completely voluntarily. There was no religion propagating it. No one forced it on people. It spread because if you learned how to use fire you were better off.

On the other hand, everyone not adopting fire would just be stupid. And when I say stupid, I mean it in the same sense as dropping a huge stone on your foot is stupid. It hurts you and most likely you end up lame.

If you were the one mutilating yourself by dropping boulders on your feet, you were not likely to be copied by other people. Becoming lame does not add value. But using fire did.

In the first days, the inventors paid a price for what they invented. With fire, the cost involved included all the accidents on the way. Most likely, the inventors burned stuff they wished would not have burned. The cost included the ridicule of others and the loathing of some.

But when the fire-makers became successful, the movement grew and became accepted. Even after all the costs involved, the inventors were better off. If they didn't lose their lives in the process, they were more recognized as innovators and had the experience involved.

Of course, I wasn't there when people first invented fire. This is only speculation, but, at least for me, this a feasible account of what happened.

But let's look at a modern example, that of the Internet.

On the grand timeline of things, the Internet is an invention that precedes Bitcoin by only a few years.

Both the Internet and Bitcoin are revolutionary creations. With both innovations, the first adopters gained a unique standing in the society that formed. They gained status and recognition because they were in on the thing early on.

The early users of the Internet needed to pay a lot for using it. If you are old enough to remember dial-up modems or even faxes, then you get the feeling of how fast technology has advanced in just decades. In the early days, it was cumbersome for sure.

Those people who took part in the creation of the Internet, or adopted it early on, did not become wealthy through their creation. The Internet was not monetized, in the same way, that fire wasn't either.

The money they got, was an indirect consequence. It was because they were esteemed as the originators, or creators, or inventors.

With Bitcoin, here lies a distinctive difference. Those who adopted it first ended up being paid directly by the innovation itself.

All the indirect benefits, such as using Bitcoin for purchases, are just a bonus. The real "beef" is that Bitcoin rewards those who adopt it when the price is still low.

Let me inject a brief story to exemplify the rapid rise of the price of Bitcoin and the fact it benefits early adopters.

Bitcoin Pizza Day

May 22, 2010 is known and celebrated as Bitcoin Pizza Day. That is when Laszlo Hanyecz offered to pay 10,000 Bitcoins for two delivered pizzas.

A British man took Hanyecz's up on his offer. He bought two pizzas for $25 and had these delivered in exchange for the 10,000 Bitcoins.

The "Bitcoin Pizza Day" is a milestone celebration for the adoption of the cryptocurrency. This "Bitcoin pizza" was the first documented purchase of a tangible good or service using Bitcoin.

At the time, it was a bargain for the British man, because 10,000 Bitcoins were worth around $41.

Just a year later, in 2011, the price for Bitcoin was already up 258.7%. You can easily Google how the price fluctuated in the years to come. As I'm writing this in 2019, the price of that 10,000 Bitcoin is over $100 Million.

Let me now return to the main gist. How are the movements that spread the innovation financed?

Revolutionary movements and finances

Every time there has been a truly remarkable innovation, a kind of "gift from God" to the society, one that spreads easily and lifts everyone adopting it, such innovations have always spread without direct incentivization.

In other words, no one received money directly to adopt it. Yet, such innovations have always happened. "If you have a cool thing, it will happen regardless."

If you think of any successful people's movement in recent history, they could finance their cause without printing their own money. Think of the fight against Apartheid in South Africa or anything similar.

For the most, these movements seek to overthrow the system from within. Concerning finances, they function within economic terms of the organization or structure that they want to overthrow.

This, of course, is very noble. Yet, it will make your life so much more difficult.

Bitcoin in itself is not a movement. In essence, it is a piece of software. There was and still is, however, a movement associated with Bitcoin that seeks to change the world monetary system.

In this sense Bitcoin was ingenious. It started with creating the resources.

If you want to change the old money system, first, you need the resources to do it. Second, you need to have the new framework that you want the old system to transform to.

If you destroy something and without having something to install in its place, people will not trust you. They fear you will mess it up. In their mind, you may you have something, but it is not sure to work so for that reason trusting you would be a big risk.

For this reason, Bitcoin was a credible candidate for a new monetary system because it created the resources for its proponents. All the early adopters eventually became rich because of Bitcoin.

At the same time, it created the payment network and the currency that would replace the old one.

Sadly, Bitcoin has been in existence for 10 years and only managed to make like maximum a million times upside to do its owners. In terms of market capitalization, hardly anyone thinks that it has been a failure.

But what is sad is that in 10 years Bitcoin has only managed to gain about 50 million users. This number of users would be good if it still had the momentum and the number of users would grow exponentially.

Bitcoin has been and continues to be a stellar investment with 10x-100x more upside in just years. But the history already shows that it will not be the linchpin to topple and dethrone the debt money system.

The reasons for this are too many to be covered here but will be later. But Bitcoin did accomplish to create the right attitude and mindset in people.

To elaborate on why this is important, I wish to take a moment to visit the way ideas are financed in startup culture.

Lessons from monetizing ideas

In the startup world, think of someone who has become successful with their startup, exited with a multimillion-dollar paycheck, and then is building a new venture.

Using his or her connections, this startup rock star uses his connections to cherry-pick a dream team for a new venture. Let's say the team has 10 people, all of whom have great accomplishments in their field.

With a great business idea and such a competent team, the founder visits the venture capitalist.

From the venture capitalist, the founder will get a large check against a piece of paper.

On that paper is the great business idea, the reputable team, and of course a reasonable valuation. If the valuation is $100 Million, the founder will receive $25 Million from the venture capitalist, who is happy to secure quarter in a potential mover-and-shaker of the new economy or the new way of life or whatnot.

Already 20 years ago, if you had what it took, you could just walk to the people with money and monetize your very existence and ideas. With this arrangement, you get money against a share in whatever you are building.

Ten years ago, came Bitcoin. It showed that it was possible to create a network that monetizes itself without even being a profit-seeking venture. It monetized a network of trust.

With the first example, the startup financing, you monetize a share of your for-profit venture. With the second example, that of Bitcoin, you monetize the token of your network.

The network in itself is not doing anything. It just is. But still, you monetize its token. This monetization is pretty valuable. In the case of Bitcoin, the valuation is over $200 Billion.

That is more, for example, than what the nation of Estonia is worth. All that valuation for a piece of software and the network of people who are using it.

With these two examples we see, first, that if you want to make something new that can be profitable, you can monetize it before it even exists. Second, you can monetize the network itself even before it exists. And when it exists and is fully operational, it doesn't need to do anything. It is still valuable.

These are the key pieces.

Combining "startup" and "token" approaches

The value of the network with Bitcoin is limited because of the number of users.

If one would want to create the most valuable network in existence, it would be one that includes all the people in the world in it.

I've chosen to create such a network. At the end of the book, there are links for those who are interested in the venture. But here I wish to explain the concept briefly.

If you consider profit generation, you have to transcend the economic profit for a moment. The reason for this is that such a network with all the people in the world can't fall prey of financial zero-sum thinking.

When you think of economic profit, in the present system if somebody pays you money so that you gain, it means that the other one has paid the money to you. In this sense, your gain is his loss.

With our network in question, we can't think of this way. When everybody is included, pure economic profit can't be the driving force or motivation. The profit, fundamentally, has to be something other than economic.

A network that includes all people needs to draw its profit measures from people's quality of life. This means how good they feel, their personal fulfillment.

The premise of this network is to expose and dethrone the fiat money system, to provide liberty from financial slavery. As a corollary is both higher personal fulfillment in comparison to present society.

For those not trained in economics, such as vision may sound unfathomable. Then the people ask, "Okay, you are offering me a piece of the sky. I don't believe you."

Another objection may be the lack of need by the individual. When someone feels they do not need such freedom, we have to find a motive that they find appealing.

My wish is not to dwell on these here. But let us instead return to the main argument.

A network that includes all the people in the world can generate a huge profit.

As we are combining the "startup approach" and "token approach", two things come together.

The reason for the startup approach is that there is so much to be gained. This network has to be very valuable.

Also, with the token approach, this network is valuable even without any monetary gain. The value lies in it being a payment network, communication network, and trust network.

Combining these approaches, we show the people what the vision is, what is the end state when all this has happened. Now, returning to economic profit, such a network has a humongous valuation.

In a sense, we package the earth and sell it to people in pieces. The payment is made with their intention, their effort and also against legacy resources that they might own, such as old school financials.

When this process is completed, and all the people have joined the network, the old system can be absolved. The old finances do not exist anymore. We cancel them.

From the day of the institution of this new monetary arrangement, there will, for example, be no one upholding the Euro system (which never was supported by a majority of the Europeans anyway).

As a side note, all existing debt will be canceled. This will even happen automatically, as a byproduct of the currency, in which the debt was denominated, becoming worthless.

A true jubilee for all the people of the earth.

Revolution overnight—the case against gold

Every day, I have to remind myself of this vision. Yet every time it feels fresh. If people would get it already, it would be accomplished by yesterday.

Henry Ford said in 1928, some 91 years ago, "It is well enough that people of the nation do not understand our banking and monetary system, for if they did, I believe there would be a revolution before tomorrow morning."[4]

What Ford was saying is that if people knew how their currency is being created, there would be a revolution overnight.

The lack of knowledge stops the people from rising to the barricades.

I understand, in 1928, they didn't know. Even if they did, at the time the best alternative for the fiat money system would have been to go back to physical gold, which had proven useful in the eighteen-hundreds.

In the present time, in 2019, the situation is different. I wouldn't advocate going back to gold. With the monetary system, we've progressed to a

---

[4]

https://www.brainyquote.com/quotes/henry_ford_1362
94

situation where gold is not the best foundation for the monetary system.

Henry Ford saw correctly that there would be a revolution if people knew what is happening behind their backs. If people would know, there would be a revolution in this day and age, too.

Also, we have a better alternative in existence. Many consider Bitcoin a better basis for the international monetary system than the US dollar is. We, however, have a better system than Bitcoin with the network which I've explained briefly above.

In our era, the problems with and the inner workings of the fiat money system are well known. So are the possible remedies.

It is well known, especially among those interested in the topic, but all the following are already explained in layman's terms to anyone with access to the Internet:

1. What kind of "magic trick" is used to create new money in the present system.
2. How money or value can be created using a completely voluntary effort.
3. How it is possible to create an alternative payment network people use for money.
4. People who participate in it will get rich if and when it succeeds.

With this, we understand that one great motivation for people to join the new system is, of course, also financial. You will gain because the system succeeds.

Yes, everybody will gain with the new system. With the eradication of the fiat money system, everybody (except the creators of the fiat money system) will gain!

But, in general, those who join first, will benefit proportionally more than those who join later.

It is a well-known fact that with most well-received cryptocoins, the founder and the first team have become rich. Of course, due to stupidity, theft, or any other factor, these can lose their wealth at some point in time. But on a general level, the first ones are wealthy for sure.

The latecomers have not always become rich in the same sense. For example, if the coin proved out to be a scam or if you just happened to buy at the wrong point and especially sell at the wrong point.

We remember many times in Bitcoin's history that if you had made your purchase at the top, you might need to wait even a few years for the price of the coin to rise higher than what you paid originally.

It is no secret that many people have lost money with Bitcoin or any other coin. You can lose money with any financial instrument.

Can a "latecomer" become wealthy?

Let me pause for a brief personal account. I have considered myself a latecomer in Bitcoin. I first heard about the coin back in 2009 and still remember vividly hearing the news about the first Bitcoin exchange, Mt. Gox, opening in July 2010.

I heard all this, I had all the information, and yet I didn't invest. I didn't invest in 2010. I didn't invest even in 2011. I just sat on the information I had on my hands.

I witnessed how the price of bitcoin went up from 7 to 8 cents, then to 25 cents and 40 cents, and later to $1 and $32.

I felt so stupid. I was angry at myself because I just watched to mine Bitcoin or buy them at 0.5 US cents per Bitcoin.

Whilst sitting all the information I had, I watched the price of Bitcoin go up 10,000 times. And still, I was waiting.

Perhaps you have a hard time relating to my story if you've only known about Bitcoin for 1-2 years, or in the case that you bought in at $20k and now are waiting for the rates to go higher than the present $10k.

Everything that has happened with Bitcoin in the past five years was already baked in from the beginning. The essence of the code behind Bitcoin was there since the beginning.

I only consciously cracked the code in 2013. Then I saw a glimpse of what was to come.

Many questions have intrigued me along my path. What is going to happen with the Bitcoin economy? What will happen with society concerning Bitcoin? What happens to all the other coins, the altcoins?

For those interested in the historical records of how my thinking has evolved, there is a forum called bitcointalk.org, where I have more than 7,000 posts listed.

On this forum, I've expounded on these questions and topics more in detail. At the time of writing these, I was not thinking about the future of those writings. I just was fascinated by Bitcoin and found it natural to write about topics of interest.

Many of the writings were not intended to be taken seriously. I for sure didn't take myself seriously most of the time. I referred to myself as either a retired or an unemployed guy.

I was a guy with a laptop just "doing this thing." Later, when I checked back my writings, I saw many of my predictions or calculations come to pass.

I remember when Bitcoin was between $100 and $1,000 (in other words, a long time ago). To me, it felt like a mature phase I saw as the early phase of Bitcoin when it was $1. In comparison, $100 felt a lot.

I remember when Bitcoin broke $100. It was on the 1st of April 2013.

Another early Bitcoin millionaire and I went for a walk on the ice in front of Helsinki. Taking off our shirts we just absorbed sunbeams, feeling like kings of the world. After all, Bitcoin was so expensive at $100 that we could buy the world.

At the time, I felt like a latecomer. Inside, I still do. But with Bitcoin valuation at $10,000 currently, hardly anybody else would consider me a latecomer.

The same goes for any monetary network that includes everyone on the planet. If you are alive now, you won't be the last one to join. Someone is joining in after you.

The Situation as we approach 2020

What I want to emphasize is that the situation in the world today is completely ready for a change.

Theoretically, Bitcoin was an innovation the kind of which cannot be dethroned because it was the first of its kind. It was a new asset class.

What I have envisioned is a currency with an immutable public ledger (such as in Bitcoin) with, however, the new money creation managed by a trusted setup. This means that the rules are agreed-on and imposed by the community, not by technology. Also, as it grows, human discretion is involved in weekly decisions, to better adapt to the changing situations. In fact, most of the new so-called cryptocurrencies use this model already.

Currency is not intended to be like based on an algorithm. With Bitcoin, it was a clear intention that it is a trustless setup. So, when you buy Bitcoins and when you use them, you don't need to be in contact with or knowledgeable of any centralized body. Furthermore, such a body should not have the ability to change the rules.

We have seen, of course, that because it is a piece of software, it needs to be developed and somebody needs to do it. In the end, when there is a proposed change, it may be that some part of the Bitcoin ecosystem might feel that it is a good change and the other part of my field that it is not. Then there are ways how to solve these situations in practice.

This principle showcases that no matter how algorithmic your setup is, especially over time it still is dependent on human action and decisions to ensure that it continues to be like usable, even technically usable, as money.

For example, it's easy to think that Bitcoin software needs to be updated if the basic protocol of the Internet is changed. Otherwise, Bitcoin will not continue to operate as a currency system dependent on the Internet.

This is just an example that no matter how trustless Bitcoin is and how, by definition, it doesn't have a counterparty, it is still not the same thing as physical gold. Because physical gold doesn't rely on any other protocol for its existence. But Bitcoin requires that the Internet is operational.

Here the point I intend to make is that now the time has come when it is possible to make a huge change that transforms us from the control of the debt-based economy to a new merit-based, abundance-based and voluntarist economy, which wasn't possible before.

There are several important aspects to consider here.

First, Bitcoin showed us as a technology what was possible. It started this whole blockchain movement. It opened up ways how to implement this kind of decentralized ledger used to record transactions and payments—and to do it on a global scale.

Bitcoin could not have been born 10 years earlier than it did. There were too many obstacles for it to come about. For instance, network transmission speeds, storage space price, and similar factors could not permit for a Bitcoin-type of a system to run.

In theory, the code might have existed earlier, but in practice, the world wasn't technically advanced enough for the implementation.

How about today? All those obstacles and bottlenecks are not there anymore. What used to be a bottleneck, isn't one today. Each of the limiting factors has seen a leap in development.

Also, what should not be forgotten, is that Bitcoin opened the horizon concerning self-created money systems. It showed to people that it was possible to create this kind of monetary system, first, without asking anyone's permission and, second, that it was possible to use this system voluntarily.

In a sense, Bitcoin showed the world that you can create your own money and choose to use it.

To me, these two never-seen-before-in-history factors in Bitcoin really stand out, the technical and the attitudinal. Before its creation, such a feat wouldn't have been technically possible, and there wasn't a widely spread disposition in the minds of men to allow people to just start using their own money.

The world after Bitcoin is very different. At least it is so in "my bubble."

Among my friends, it is common to see "creating your own money" as a viable alternative. When friends of mine have a venture of some kind in mind, they are thinking whether to securitize or tokenize it. These are the two options.

Funny enough, these two are basically the same thing. The difference is only a matter of nuance.

Part 3 – Efficient code and other pivotal changes

At large, where are people at?

It is not just that "there is a growing number of people who understand the possibilities of cryptocurrencies." What is even more important is change of general consciousness of the people of the earth.

To preface this, I have to say that, "Yes, I know I'm not the wisest person on the earth."

The reason I can confess this easily that I'm still very aware of the speed of development in my thinking in recent years. I understand I have been wrong in so many ways. Countless times have I needed to update my understanding.

Looking back two or three years, I consider myself at the time as an infant, with regard to economic thinking. Sure, I had my training in economics, successes in business and all the accolades. But all that weighs very little in the scales.

Since then, my thinking has evolved in leaps and bounds.

I used to see vague and blurry, but now my gaze is sharp. To draw an analogy from cameras, I have more pixels and the lights are much brighter.

This discernment is very valuable to me. I can confess that in my past, I really did not understand people well. Especially, if I compare my skills then and now, the difference is enormous.

My focus and interest have always been in concepts. Not events, not people but concepts or the codification.

I have studied a little coding with programming languages as part of my education in Helsinki University of Technology (now: Aalto University) in the early 2000s. But I do not practice these, because I can do most of my necessary coding in spreadsheets. (There are, of course, always other people who can implement the code I've envisioned.)

Sure, in a sense I feel hesitant when somebody says they have studied programming for 10 years and then worked professionally for 20 more years for some big companies and a fat 100k paycheck. Yet the results of many of those big projects seem laughable.

In Finland, the software development endeavors of the national railway company or national healthcare services are both a laughingstock.

Somehow it takes 50 million Euros to develop a platform for selling tickets for an obscure railway company. It sells thousands of tickets per day.

Yet honestly, I just can't figure out how it is even possible to make it so difficult. I mean, if I would need to specify a train ticket pricing and selling solution with all the features that are humanly needed, it would never take more than €100,000 to implement it.

How can these guys spend 50 million and take three years to do it? If I had known that it would be three years to do it, I would personally have implemented it in using nothing else except Google sheets. It would have taken me a maximum of two months.

(And yes, I would have asked a €100,000 paycheck for that time for doing it. But not more.)

Usually, I don't speak or write about these topics. But they need to be addressed.

The difference whether you are coding in a smart or in a not-so-smart way is huge. It is breathtaking that those people who are regarded professionals are the ones who are working for big companies and a big paycheck. Funny enough, they are being paid to code in a non-efficient way.

Then there are others who are paid based on output. They are paid based on results.

I'll take a personal example to illustrate this point.

The code for a car-sharing business

Back in the days, in 2004, I started the first in the world car-sharing company that had the feature that the cars don't need to be booked in advance.

In this car-sharing system, the car was an object that you could contract to your use if it happened to be ready and available. If someone else was using it, you could not contract it. But once the other person checked the car out, it was available for others to reserve for immediate use.

So, no advance requirements. The operating principle was that you can just flexibly take the car at a time of need.

The biggest advantages for this operation mode are threefold.

First of all, you never pay more than what you use. This is huge. You don't need to know in advance how long you will need the car or how many kilometers you are going to drive.

In the opposite scenario, you needed to guess your needs in advance, and you were penalized for not guessing accurately. This is a massive inefficiency.

Second, having those advance bookings fragments the cars' operating schedule so that the effective use time is a much lower percentage of total time. When someone wants to make a new booking, the other bookings need to be considered.

Third, this is much easier. When you need a car, you'll just check whether the car is there. Then you reserve it, take it and return or leave it.

All this happened in 2004 and it was the first such car-sharing system in the world. And now I'm getting to my main point again: The efficiency of code.

This software having all of these features plus a variable pricing model based on the demand and load situation (same way as with many of the airlines today).

Of course, it had the client database, billing systems, customer account management, complete admin features, messaging, and so on. The normal stuff you'd expect in a system of this magnitude.

I would say that the total difficulty level might have been at par with the railway company's ticketing software. The main difference was that for us, the specifications and coding for this software until a full one hundred percent production capability took us three months (instead of three years!) and the cost was 800 Euros.

No, I'm not kidding. That was the real time frame and that was the real cost. Contracted from the same

guys at commercial prices instead of student &
friend discounted ones, it'd still have been less than
€5,000. The venture was called Autopooli and
operated in the Helsinki University of Technology's
campus in 2004-2007.

Keep it simple (and effective)

When you know what you are doing, you get great
results habitually. Others can try the same thing and
waste resources to come up with a really bad result.

The one who knows his stuff considers it "normal"
to make solutions that are just more to the point
than the other alternative solutions. That it is just
normal.

But what is not normal is the inefficiency we see
with much of the "enterprise software." As if size
and complexity would give a valid reason for
inefficiency! Many of the solutions at use in the
world are not the best solutions but, on the
contrary, the worst possible solutions for the very
issue.

Where is the root of the problem? After all, many of
these problem cases would be easy to conceptualize.
Let's take money, for instance.

With computer games, the programmers and game
designers are not economists or some other

"monetary scientists." So, when computer games have money, they don't make it too complicated.

In most games, the concept and role of money are very clear. It is a measure of wealth and a means of payment.

The money that a player has can be marked with a number. Normal mathematics works just fine. One billion is more than one million, and so on. Both are more than one thousand.

As a measure of wealth, the more money you have the better. How much is there? Just read the number.

The other issue was payments. In a payment, you give some of these numbers on your account to the account of another person. You specify to whom to give and how much. Then, your measure (or, in other words, your account) grows smaller and the other grows bigger, respectively.

Again, this is no "advanced mathematics." Just addition and subtraction, what you learn in elementary school.

With the annual game awards and honors of different kinds, never has there been an occasion that a game would be lauded for the "monetary innovations in the multiplayer online game, allowing players to store their wealth on their account, make real-time payments to other players without delay or transfer costs."

Having an in-game money system that works is not the goal. It is the floor.

If someone were to design an in-game money system that resembles the real world, you would need to pay tens of dollars just to do a payment, and it would take up to two weeks to see the money on the receiver's account.

No one even tries to design such games because the gaming community wouldn't know whether to cry or laugh.

With in-game money systems, the baseline is that transfers are immediate and don't cost anything.

Yet, with real-world societies in general, it is completely different. We don't see such development.

Instead, millions of people are professionally employed worldwide by this "money transferring system called 'finance and banking'" that does not even work.

Finding your role

During my formative years, people always told me to "get a job," but I felt an aversion to such. I didn't see myself as just doing a small part in a big thing. I felt I wouldn't make a good soldier when I should be the one commanding the generals.

Well, of course, that is one of the challenges in the old legacy society. If you are smart enough to be commanding the generals, you still won't get to that position easily, because everything works through hierarchies.

The path to commanding generals is that first, you have to be a good soldier to become a non-commissioned officer (NCO). As an NCO, you need to be very smart to get to the officer's school. And so on.

I did my compulsory military service in Pori Brigade, Finland in 1999-2000, serving in the recently established elite military unit Rapid Deployment Force (RDF). This unit was notable for being UN and NATO compatible.

(20 years later, Finland is still not officially a member of NATO, because 80% of the population stubbornly refuses to see its benefits (pun intended). Instead, a Host Nation Agreement[5] is in place to align Finland with the NATO war effort.)

---

[5] The official name of this treasonous paper: *"Memorandum of understanding (MOU) between the government of the Republic of Finland and Headquarters, Supreme Allied Commander Transformation as well as Supreme Headquarters Allied Powers Europe regarding the provision of Host Nation Support for the execution of NATO operations / exercises / similar military activity"* is

The nine months in the army presented me with a snapshot of the different layers of society. As the military service is compulsory in Finland and, especially 20 years ago when I did my military service, it was difficult to avoid it. Therefore, in the army, you see all the different strata of society.

You see the smart ones, the stupid ones, the misfits, and all.

The stupid ones are used for cannon fodder. The smart ones are put into the NCO training and then to officer school and so on. The misfits end up as drivers or medics or other supporting roles.

Many of the misfits would, in fact, be great generals or high officers. But they hate all the steps leading to that position and would not function well in them.

The misfits would make poor NCOs, for example. The NCOs are the end of the chain of command. They need to enforce whatever they are told to do and lead the troops by example.

If you are a misfit, you just hate having someone above you, someone more stupid than you are, giving you orders and making you tell your friends what to do. You might feel that the person and the commands are completely stupid, but there is nothing you can do about it.

---

carefully worded to not claim a shred of legal process in creating it, for there was none.

In the army, the ones who have great capabilities other than "just following orders" are disqualified from the get-go. Nowadays, most of these people don't even try to enter the army because there is the option of choosing civil service (or, of course, doing jail time as a "total objector", i.e. for refusing military and non-military service of your country).

This is instructive, because the same thing happens in general society. Or, to be more exact, let's say it "used to happen" because we are more and more entering the era when the system has cracks in it.

If you go back 20 years, when I was making these choices, or if you go back 40 years, your options were much more limited. Therefore, the smart people were disqualified early on in their career and they were basically finished.

How does this disparity play off in society? If I look at the top people in any arena, when assessing the top skilled, or top creative people, many of them are piss broke. They have incredibly little money.

Only those who have been able to monetize their ideas in the way of startups or who are artists – such as musicians – can make some money, at least occasionally.

But in general, the most creative people are often experiencing a salary gap. They are paid far less than people without any creativity at all.

How could it be achieved that the top creatives would not lack finances or other resources? How could it come to pass that the people with the most potency to affect the world could gain the resources to do it?

This is something I see changing in the future. And it's sooner than one might think.

Finding the "Third Way"

I mentioned the car-sharing business earlier. But if we take this idea a bit further and dream for a moment.

What if all the cars in the world would be shared? Then, you could just walk down the street, find the first car that you like (and that is not in use), click a button on your mobile phone to reserve it, jump in and drive it wherever you want to?

If this is far-fetched for you, well, in China there are "car vending machines," that are stacked with new cars in an elevator system. If you want to test drive one, you can reserve it with your mobile phone, pick it up, and drive it around for three days for the cost or around $50 or even free with a good social score.[6]

---

[6] I won't comment here on the problems of China's social scoring system but just want to highlight the ease of use made possible by technology. More on the vending machine:

But let's return to that dream of having all the cars of the world plugged into a system of sharing. Everybody pays based on how much they use the cars – measured by the length of use in time, distance travelled, fuel use, or even the "quality" of one's driving.

If you think of car ownership, the first way is privatized. That basically means that everybody owns their own car.

The second way is socialism. That means, "let's socialize all the cars," and "everybody can just ride the cars and they don't need to be maintained." Well, that does not work.

But the third way is that people realize voluntarily the benefits of the system.

The car-sharing networks are a great example. No one is forcing people to participate, but more and more do because it makes sense. It makes sense financially, it makes sense environmentally, it makes sense in so many different ways.

Networks such as this are just springing up. The car-sharing systems are the third way. I mean, they are commercially operated entities.

---

https://techcrunch.com/2018/03/25/ford-and-alibaba-unveil-car-vending-machine/

What makes in-game economies so efficient? Well, the game designers had no agenda making them difficult. They didn't have a concept of a difficult monetary system but a simple one.

They didn't need to make it difficult just to control people. They had all the control they could want anyway – after all, they could see everybody's balances and review their transactions at any time.

In the same way with car-use and car-ownership, if you just ignore aspects of "displaying your status as a car owner", and just consider "getting from A to B," the simplest way is just to hail a taxi or commission the nearest shared car.

The example of non-shared cars is an example of bad design. It is a huge global drag on economy and also destroying the planet in a factual way.

Our life as a digital information layer

All banking solutions are designed with their basic feature in mind: sending money from one person to another.

Let us study, what is needed to accomplish such transactions and the needed systems most economically.

With that said, it is not just a question of efficiency. If we are "programming the world," let us include as a goal to make the digital information layer of human existence, one that actually serves humans.

So, if we were to design the information layer of human existence, starting from scratch, how would we do it? Can it even be done? And if successful in designing this, what will happen when people like it and start using it?

The goal therefore is to design the most effective software to accomplish this. This, for some, may sound so simple that it sounds even naïve to some.

Some don't believe that it would be possible to write the code for a very simple software. And, as we saw before, the world is full of exceedingly complex software that do their job very poorly or fail at it completely. Isn't it possible to succeed in the opposite?

The reasoning for "you can't design something simple to solve something complex" seems like a psychological illusion.

First, people think it's easier to make a software that is terribly complicated and difficult to use. On top, they think it's somehow impossible to make a software that is simple, efficient in its operations, and intuitive to use.

This is so laughable. What I've done all my adult life is design software. I don't write the code, but I design the structures and functions. That is what I've done for the past 18 years.

To begin to design a piece software, I will start from the requirements. I look at what is required from the software and then find out the easiest way to do it.

This is basic requirements analysis: Get clear on everything the software needs to do. These are the requirements. Then, design the best way to get the job done.

Let's start with the basics and use the analogy of children. They are a great example. In general, kids have less baggage compared to adults. Observing them learn is therefore of great benefit.

Of course, people want some level of difficulty in their lives. Overcoming difficulties – problems, adversities, and challenges – adds great meaning to life. However, being challenged by poorly functioning information systems is not such a difficulty one seeks to overcome. It brings no growth, just irritation.

What do kids want? It starts with food and shelter. When they grow up, they also want to transact with other kids.

"I have these marbles and candy. Why don't we barter?"

When they grow a little bit older, they might want to take a bus to visit a friend. For this reason, they need money and tickets.

By this we see, that the needs might become more complex, but the basic foundation remains the same.

Let me elaborate more on this information layer.

If you are flying to a location with an airplane, well, the airplane itself is a physical thing. You might say it makes up the physical layer. The plane is what does the actual flying.

The information layer marks who gets to sit where, who pays the gasoline used, and so on.

The basic feature is authentication. The software needs to know who is using it.

Second is you need to manage your possessions. You need a medium of exchange.

(At the moment, there is way to exist and transact without such a medium. We need money.)

Since you have money, you can technically have everything else that resides in the information layer.

In the information layer, the cost of recording the ownership of one marble, a million marbles or a billion marbles, is the same."

For banking solutions, it's about "sending money"

In a bank's account management software, such as your online bank or banking application on your mobile phone, the main feature there is sending money. That is what is most needed.

But, when you think of it, you can do the same with any virtual item, not just money. The difference between money or any other virtual item is smaller than you think; there isn't really any.

What else do we need in this virtual layer of human existence? Of course, there has to be communication. Especially recorded communication.

By the simplest definition, by recorded communication I mean everything except face-to-face communication. This can be anything that historically has been recorded, such as books or audio or video, for example phone calls.

Of course, books and sheet music and what not exist in physical form, but what we are mostly interested in is the digital information.

If you were to assess the different digital communications you use, this is a simple way to do it.

In your everyday life, record all the times that you use a digital instrument, such as your phone, tablet, or computer. Record also, what was the key reason for you to use the tool, and whether or not you were able to complete your task with the most sensible and efficient manner.

Of course, many forms of communication are very difficult to make better. In general, phone calls are one form of communication that it hasn't really been improved in the past 50, if not 100 years.

Many things have been tried like video calls, but most people are not using it. Then again, if you look at it from the point of view of the deaf and the mute, video calls are a huge improvement; without them they would not be able to communicate so well.

Other things are much easier to improve. An example of this is customs declarations. For some reason, they still seem like a torturing device not intended to help the users.

Also, the need for a customs declaration is from my point of view completely arbitrary. But if it has to be, then it could be done much more efficiently.

When we think what we as humans need from a digital existence, and how certain building blocks stack on top of each other and complement each other, it "clicks."

For example, when you have authentication that really works, people are happy to have it on all the time. That is the reason, in part, that people are happy to have Google and Facebook spy on them all the time, because they enjoy the convenience of "logging in with Facebook" or "logging in with Google."

What if there were a solution where you would not be forced to give away your privacy and still have your need met? What if you would not need to expose yourself to all the ads and have these giants sell your information to third parties?

That, in fact, is what banks do, too. They give you a means of authentication – but in exchange, you have to be part of the system. You have to play their game, a game rigged against you.

Well, that was only a side note.

When we have authentication that really works, most people would be happy to have it on all the time. Then, for example, when they book a flight ticket or something different.

In a sense, the question is about "reorganizing the world."

Sharing economy and ownership

As I'm walking down the street, I see all these resources, all this tangible wealth. There are houses, and there are cars.

When I was a kid, I didn't have a good concept of ownership. Or, the one I had was very limited. It only extended the reach of my arms. I owned what I could carry or have in front of me.

Everything else, such as my parents' professions, were "stuff that I could use." On the other hand, there were things I couldn't use, such as my neighbors' possessions.

As kids we see the world in a different way. Is there something we could learn from that?

What if we could take some of that way of seeing the world and introduce it back to the adults?

What if we take the physical world as granted but liberate it to shared use through the informational layer?

If you look at the buildings in a city's center, many of them are empty most of the time. Very seldom they are used for anything – at least anything fun.

But what if they would? If you could commission anything that you see to your use? And to have a single app to do it?

Yes, I know this may seem utopian, but bear with me.

If we were to design such an informational layer on reality, we would not need to force it on people. We would only need to design it in a way that provides the Minimum Viable Solution. We need something functional that some people can start using it.

There are countless examples – Uber, Amazon, and so on. I don't really need to name these.

There are countless of inventions or innovations where information is processed in a better way than before. Many of such startups are worth billions already.

But when you combine all such features and do so with a visionary mindset and get the thing off the ground, my thesis is that it will go viral. And it will transform the whole world.

Not only will it transform the world, but it will do so without interfering with the people's rights, such as right to ownership.

Or course, it works best when people are not adamant about or on the defense just making sure their ownership is protected. Just like with the kids, it's much easier to play with people who are willing and eager to share.

But in the starting phase, we can manage it strictly the same as Uber and Amazon. They are functioning in a competitive marketplace.

Whenever we are able to do away with regulations, that will be wonderful. But in the beginning, it is not like that. Some regulators will want to impose rules on us. To some extent, we need to comply.

But the main point is this: Even then, there is so much potential to make the world better by rethinking all of it.

When you think of it, there are so many technologies out there. I'm not even talking too much of new technologies to come but those in existence. Neither am I talking about building complicated technologies.

But, instead, I'm talking about building the existence from the simple premises of

1. who you are,
2. what do you have, and
3. what are the things that you can do?

All great inventions start off simple. Then they grow to more complex expressions, but the core remains the same.

Conclusion

Having seen the problems in the current money system, you and I know that is bound to change sooner or later.

Whenever a dominant system is overthrown, some people benefit from it massively.

In the past, it has not been possible to monetize a paradigm-shift in such a profound way. When the Internet was created, people who first used it had an advantage, yet they still needed to pay for that privilege.

The invention of the Internet was so powerful that I don't really need to elaborate on it. But, in a nutshell, the Internet and the resulting access to all the knowledge, news and people, is more valuable than everything (material) that I own.

And I don't own the Internet! The value is there without anyone owning it, as it was with all the innovations and with everything else, ever since the beginning of our manufactured history, up until... Bitcoin.

Bitcoin was the first innovation that contained the mechanism for incentivizing people to use it by rewarding them for the use, instead of requiring them to pay for it.

The first mobile phones? Clumsy and expensive, yet the ones buying and using them, got a distinct advantage. Now everyone uses them.

First social media? Clumsy, yet free. Those who were there in the beginning, hold positions of influence now.

First cryptocurrency? Clumsy, but ... *you actually got rich merely by being there.*

The advantages of the utility, the innovation itself, were in a sense "just a great bonus."

Pay heed now, this might be the most important thing you hear in your life. And you heard it from me first:

<u>It is possible to monetize the whole new level of existence in the same way as Bitcoin</u>, by awarding the value of the end state, to the participants during the process of creating the end state. It seems more complicated if you don't know.

But as my mentor said with Bitcoin: *"It does not matter if you understand or not. It matters if you buy in or not."*

When the System is overthrown or transforms, the first movers benefit the most.

How can you be among those early adopters?

First, you can buy in not only with your legacy financial wealth. Those who see what is valuable in the future are happy to exchange away what is valuable only at the moment.

Second, you can buy in with your time and effort (example here with the lopsided well-being bonus).

Third, you can get your share just by the decision to join. Even with no legacy money, you can be among the first movers.

Fourth, a friend of yours can buy you in. If you are hesitating, a good friend will help you through the door. (You can thank that person later.)

Everyone will force their way in. And in the end, everyone will be in. And many of the first will become the last. Because they were busy thinking they owned the Earth, whereas in fact,

the Earth is being inherited by the righteous as we speak.

Next steps

Let other people know of this book

Thank you so much for being a finisher! You read the book until the end.

I'd like to ask you for a favor. Would you consider taking 2 minutes and writing your review on Amazon?

Just write briefly, what you liked best about the book, who you think would benefit from reading it, and if you have some ideas to make it better.

I'd love to hear your feedback "fresh off the bat" as you just went through it. With your help, I hope to make future versions of the book even better.

I have a surprise for everyone who writes me reader feedback. You can send your comments to dragon@dragonspeaks.io and I'll send you my surprise gift.

(Please allow me some time to respond, as I read all of these personally.)

See what I'm up to

To get my latest podcasts, books and videos, go to my personal website, dragonspeaks.io.

If you didn't yet watch the keynote presentation I promised, you can do so here: www.dragonspeaks.io/keynote

Application guides for the book and other online resources

If you read the book, and would like to put these ideas to practice, I've compiled guides and tools to help with that. You can find these here: www.dragonspeaks.io/your-reward

About the author

Risto Pietilä, a.k.a. The Dragon is a serial entrepreneur, economist, and a Bitcoin millionaire. He became a millionaire before the age of thirty, and through several successes in business, has secured financial freedom. Now, he is dedicated to helping others achieve liberation as well.

Mr. Pietilla's ability to reach Millionaire status before he turned thirty was a culmination of formative experiences as a young adult growing up in Finland.

Early life and education

During his teens, Risto Pietilä was among the top of the youth in his country. He attended the historical highschool of Hämeenlinna, the alma mater of the 7th President of Finland, J. K. Paasikivi, and internationally well-known Finnish composer, Jean Sibelius.

In the 1990s, Pietilä was selected for several youth exchange programs, for example, in Italy, Japan, Thailand, and Australia. (This was extremely rare for anyone in Finland in the 1990s.)

Pietilä ranked in top-4 in the national Chemistry competition all the three years he attended, won the Mental arithmetic competition all the 3 years he attended and was twice a Chemistry Olympiad delegate, once scoring a bronze medal. He graduated from high school with 5 *laudatur*, roughly translated "praised" or "lauded." This is the highest grade that the authorities award to the top 5% of students per subject in the Finnish Matriculation examination yearly.

Pietilä has a wide experience from the Finnish Defense Forces. He served his 9-month compulsory military service in voluntary special forces unit Pori Brigade, Rapid Deployment Force (combined field, APC driver, UN, and Nato military/"peacekeeper" training). He was recognized in his unit with the most "kuntoisuusloma" (extracurricular leave granted based on personal achievements). After his service time, Pietilä continued his studies at the Helsinki University of Technology, Department of Industrial Engineering and Management.

Because of his success in the national Chemistry competition and the Matriculation examination, Pietilä would have been able to enter several universities with no entrance examination. He rejected the grant from the Helsinki School of Economics but majored in Economics in the Helsinki University of Technology (now: Aalto University). His chosen degree program was in the Department of Industrial Engineering and Management, which continues to be the highest esteemed program of the school (entrants are the top 0.1% of all applying students).

Pietilä took part in the Mensa IQ test in 2003, scoring 167 points. Soon afterward, he became a conscientious-objector-in-reserve and has not taken part in NATO military exercises since 2000 (South Norway).

Business life and investing

Pietilä co-founded his first company at 20, after less than a year of studies. The company, Jamera Networks (nowadays Jamera) reached the operational capability of 80 simultaneous buy/sell teams deployable in any location in the country in addition to having about 10 fixed locations in Finland. Pietilä's involvement discontinued in a corporate ouster in 2003. Local authorities recognized as the most profitable in Central Finland in ~2011.

After those hectic years, Pietilä took some distance from the intense and fully immersed startup life. He got married and devised other business ideas. One of these ideas was the world's first system of car rental based on immediate car takeover upon need, meaning no bookings. This company, Autopooli Oy, was operational several years before Uber came to the market. Pietilä, however, discontinued the concept to transition into another highly lucrative market.

In 2006 Pietilä saw the financial crisis approaching and paid airtime to get his voice heard through a new national alternative TV-channel "Heaven TV7" of which he had previously cornered 1.5% of ownership. The 3-hour live TV show became so successful that the station aired it repeatedly. Pietilä has since been featured both on radio and TV in "crisis watch" programs. He has been featured in every Finnish TV channel plus the whole page in the largest newspaper.

The same year Pietilä began dealing in physical investment metals. The business got bigger only in 2008 after some free publicity from the government of Finland. Connected to these activities, Pietilä has co-owned and co-operated hopea.fi (2006-2013), Scenario Investments Oy (2006-2010), Eesti Investeerimishõbe OÜ (2009-), Silverbank (2010-2016), Crypto Holding (2010-). More than 100 people have invested in Pietilä's companies over 15 years and they have had over 100,000 clients. The market cap of the companies is one to a few million euros each.

A thought leader in cryptocurrencies

With silver investing, Pietilä became a Euro millionaire before he was thirty. It secured him a position that would later be multiplied in the cryptocurrency scene. Knowing about cryptocurrencies since the beginning, Pietilä has selected Bitcoin, Monero and Crypto Kingdom to be his picks. They are massively on the black compared to thousands of other coins which turned out to be scams.

Pietilä's trading skills included profitable Bitcoin price manipulation, especially until the end of 2013. With Monero, the first privacy coin, Pietilä's bullish buying caused most of the price spikes in the charts for the first two years of Monero's existence. This, however, was not for manipulative reasons but just mere confidence in the coin made him buy it at then-record prices. Some industry professionals and members of the cryptocurrency media have counted Pietilä among the TOP-100 in the worldwide cryptocurrency scene.

Over a full 20 years, Pietilä has written over 10,000 posts in message boards, blogs, and related media. On Bitcointalk alone he wrote over 7,000 posts. Pietilä is holiday-proficient in 8 languages and writes academically in English and occasionally Finnish (the latter being his native language).